My Walk WITH CHRIST

Barbara Buononato

My Walk with Christ

Copyright © 2022 Barbara Buononato

All rights reserved. No part of this book may be reproduced or transmitted in any form or by any means without the written permission of the author.

Scriptures marked KJV are taken from the KING JAMES VERSION (KJV): KING JAMES VERSION, public domain.

Scripture taken from the New King James Version®. Copyright © 1982 by Thomas Nelson. Used by permission. All rights reserved.

Scripture quotations marked (NIV) are taken from the Holy Bible, New International Version®, NIV®. Copyright © 1973, 1978, 1984, 2011 by Biblica, Inc.™ Used by permission of Zondervan. All rights reserved worldwide. www.zondervan.com. The "NIV" and "New International Version" are trademarks registered in the United States Patent and Trademark Office by Biblica, Inc.™.

Scriptures marked AMP are taken from the AMPLIFIED BIBLE (AMP): Scripture taken from the AMPLIFIED® BIBLE, Copyright © 1954, 1958, 1962, 1964, 1965, 1987 by the Lockman Foundation Used by Permission. (www.Lockman.org)

Published by:
Eleviv Publishing Group
Centerville, OH 45458
info@elevivpublishing.com
www.elevivpublishing.com

ISBN: 978-1-952744-49-5 (PB)
     978-1-952744-53-2 (E-book)

Printed in the United States of America

Table of CONTENTS

Introduction

Chapter 1: At the Beginning 7

Chapter 2: My First Christian Experience 13

Chapter 3: Life in the United States of America 20

Chapter 4: Trying Out a Second Time 27

Chapter 5: The Healing Hands of Jehovah Rapha 35

Chapter 6: Sharing My Testimony with The World 42

Chapter 7: A Wonderful Family of Christ 48

Chapter 8: Liberating My Beloved Family from Bondage 55

Chapter 9: It Is a Free Gift for All 79

Chapter 10: Fulfilling the Requirements of Salvation of Man .. 90

Chapter 11: After Salvation, What Next? 100

DEDICATION

I dedicate this book to God and my husband, Glenn, for believing in me and my walk with Jesus.

ACKNOWLEDGEMENT

It takes a large crowd to help even a small book to be made; the completion of this book could not have been possible without the help of Jesus Himself. Accordingly, I would like to acknowledge my Heavenly Father first for being my continuous inspiration throughout the writing of this book. He brought back to my remembrance all the events related herein. Secondly, a debt of gratitude is owed to my husband Glenn for witnessing, encouraging, and testifying to this day my successful transition from the Hindu faith to becoming a disciple of Christ. I appreciate his support, without which this project would have dragged on and on without completion.

I also want to thank my spiritual mother, Apostle Queen Belema Abili, for teaching me daily how to love God with all my heart. She was the instrument God used to bring better meaning to my journey through the period covered in this book. Thanks to her leadership and obedience to God, the guidance and discipline she built up in me were the driving force that made it all happen. Lastly, I want to thank my daughters Christine, Melissa, and Meghan for always supporting me in my Christian walk.

Who is He, this King of glory?

   The LORD Almighty—

   He is the King of glory.

Psalms 24:10 (NIV)

INTRODUCTION

My walk with Christ is a book about supernatural healing. Not only physical healing but also spiritual. It is a brief exposition of my meeting and falling in love with Jesus despite my Hindu background. It tells of how Jesus saved me despite my shortcomings, healed me, and gave me an important assignment towards the deliverance of my family members from the bondage of worshiping false gods.

I give God all the glory due Him; without Him, this vision would never have happened. He instructed His prophetess and prophets to prophesy to me about writing my book with the knowledge and wisdom He has given me.

As you journey with me through the chapters of this book, I believe you will be truly blessed in Jesus' name.

The LORD makes firm the steps
  of the one who delights in him;
though he may stumble, he will not fall,
  for the Lord upholds him with His hand.
Psalms 37:23-24 (NIV)

Chapter One

At The Beginning.

My name is Barbara Buononato, and I was born into a Hindu family to my wonderful parents, Tulunce and Pinky Singh of Dundee, Mahaicony, on the East Coast of the Demerara River in the country of Guyana. I am the fourth child of my parents. Mine was a fairly conservative family growing up, and talking about Jesus Christ or Christianity was forbidden in our Hindu home. Growing up in a third-world country limited my chances and abilities to do everything I dreamt of doing in life. I dreamt of achieving remarkable things and visiting beautiful places as a child. I thought of growing up to be extraordinarily successful and being a blessing not only to my family and community but to my country. Even though I had limited access to information and education, I heard about people who achieved beautiful things in life, and I aspired to one day be spoken about like those people.

However, I was to discover firsthand later that, at times in life, success can be a function of one's environment and background.

Achieving incredible feats in life is not just about dreaming but waking up to put forward some effort towards achieving your dream. Such effort could mean a bold step of faith to leave your immediate environment.

Growing up in my country was not so easy. At some point, living was getting hard in that third-world country to the extent that day-to-day survival became a task. The men go out daily to work, and the women stay home to take care of the home and garden. Resources were getting scarce with limited job opportunities. Many people grow up with little or no education and without formal knowledge of any form of trade. They resort to menial jobs that may not fetch enough to cater to their needs and the needs of their families.

Another negative factor to the whole issue is the culture of women not going out to work. They mostly stay at home, taking care of the home and small gardens of food crops around the house. These women never amount to much in life apart from bearing children. In their old age, they have little things to say about what they had done with their lives. These are some of my motivations as a youth to make something meaningful I could talk about later in life.

As a result of idleness and poor birth control, many give birth to more children than they can care for, further compounding their problems. The children grow up ignorant and continue the tradition of ignorance within the same third-world setting.

The health care system was also inferior, leading to the deaths of women, especially during childbirth. The death rate of infants was relatively high, and it all painted a picture of gloom and doom. When intertribal frictions happen, the women and the children suffer more as expected.

The country of Guyana is made up of several people who practice different religions. The predominant religions in the country were Hindu and Islam. The vast difference in religious beliefs, too, was not without its challenges. People tend to see things differently owing to their different religious beliefs, which slow down the chance of collective success. Several people also believe their religion was the better, either directly or indirectly condemning the faiths of others. This attitude puts a strain on the way people relate and work together.

Worse still, despite the terrible trend of inter-religious rifts, there were also issues of tribal sentiments.

The different tribes secretly harbor resentment toward the

other tribes, and things got terrible in the country in the late seventies. It got so bad that the Black people started killing the Indians; this resulted in those affected trying to get out of the country, leaving behind everything they had worked so hard for. Most affected people had nowhere to run to, leaving them to face a life of uncertainty and a constant risk of death in their homeland. It was a terrible situation in the country in those trying days.

The good news is that in recent times things have started turning for the better. The level of awareness and intertribal tolerance is increasing, among other things. However, when I was growing up, it was not so. At some point, I started dreaming of an opportunity to one day travel out of the country in the hope of finding peace amidst plenty.

Luckily for my family, we had a relative abroad who was willing to help us out of the carnage breaking out all around us at home. I had an aunt who resided in the United States of America. As a result of the incessant killings of people of my tribe and the report reaching her, my aunt made a permanent arrangement for us to relocate to the United States of America to be with her.

It took her a while but eventually, she was able to arrange our papers to come to the United States of America,

Leaving Guyana for the United States of America aroused many mixed feelings in my mind. We had to leave behind everything we knew, our house, the beautiful hills, the people we used to relate with, and so on, which hurts. On the other hand, life in the United States of America provided us with freedom and a higher survival chance coupled with ease of finding a means of livelihood, unlike what we obtained back home in Guyana. Despite the sentimental attachment to my home country, it was not difficult choosing to relocate to the USA rather than to continue staying in my home country with all the attending risks.

As was often the case, we could not all leave Guyana simultaneously. My parents and two of my siblings came to the United States of America about twenty-nine years ago. Some time ago, my dad passed away at a ripe old age here in the United States of America, but my mom is still alive and very much with us. My journey away from home and into a new reality in the USA began at eighteen. It is a journey that took me through several difficulties, but I am grateful today for what God has taken me through.

For I am the Lord your God

who takes hold of your right hand

and says to you, Do not fear;

I will help you.

Isaiah 41:13 (NIV)

Chapter Two

My First Christian Experience.

My journey to knowing Christ up close and the attending experiences all began on a particular night. On a Friday night, I was on my way home after a two-and-a-half-hour train ride from New York City to Poughkeepsie Train Station. I alighted from the train full of life, though quite weary from sitting down for so long. I found my way to the car park and got into my car to head home. It was a familiar route for me, through a normal path due to my job. Unknown to me, that night's experience would be different.

For better understanding, let me tell you my story of growing up in a typical Hindu home. You see, I am the fourth child of my parents. They had six children, including me: four girls and two boys.

Just as growing up in a typical Christian religious household means attending church services every Sunday and some weekdays, celebrating every Hindu religious activity was all I knew growing up. But deep down inside my heart, I got to know and fell in love with the Name 'Jesus.'

I could not tell my parents how I felt about Jesus or the Christian religion; they would have flogged some Hindu sense back into my head.

The grass withers and the flowers fall,
   but the word of our God endures forever.
Isaiah 40:8 (NIV)

On Easter day of 1974, my grandparents visited my parents in Dundee, Mahaicony East Coast Demerara Guyana, and asked me to stay with them during the Easter recess from school. They then lived in the countryside at their place located in the East Berbice-Corentyne Region of Guyana, a considerable distance from my parent's house. I was excited at the opportunity to stay with them in the countryside for some time. I was about twelve years of age then. I returned with them, hoping to catch all the fun that life in the countryside could offer. There was an exciting surprise awaiting me.

My grandfather (without the knowledge of my parents) used to host a weekly Sunday school service and Bible study for teenagers in his yard.

Guyana is below the equator, so it is a hot climate country. As a result, it was more convenient having a Sunday school service gathering outdoors within the yard rather than indoors.

I saw some teenagers entering the yard on my first Sunday morning with my grandparents. I found their presence puzzling as it did not seem like they were doing so for the first time. Rather than me challenging them, they were the ones looking at me like a stranger in the yard. I quickly went to look for my grandfather. When I finally found him in his room, he was dressed and ready for Sunday school and Sunday service.

I was a bit taken aback seeing him all dressed up so early in the morning on the weekend. I wondered where he was going. I thought of asking him but decided to put that aside for a more important question concerning the visitors in the yard. Still breathless from rushing around looking for him, I told my grandpa that I saw some people, primarily teenagers coming into the yard. He smiled and said that Sunday School was about to start and that I should get dressed too.

I cannot say which one got the better of me: was it the surprise of knowing my grandfather was conducting a Christian religious activity in his yard?

Or was it the excitement of getting a chance to experience such an activity myself? All I knew was that I was overly excited and wanted to see what it was all about.

My grandfather got the teenagers and me together in a row, and he started to pray, and when he mentioned the name of Jesus, I began to weep. The tears just started flowing without my control. I felt so overwhelmed with emotion; I knew it had to do with that name, "Jesus." The feeling was so different from what I had ever experienced before. Even though I was merely twelve years of age, I could tell that there was something special about that name, "**Jesus**."

I did not want him to know that I was crying, so I held most of it inside of me. Then they started singing, "Jesus took my burden and rolled them in the sea." Here again, the name of Jesus was mentioned. I could hardly hold myself anymore. I love the name of Jesus so much, and I could scarcely stand hearing it without that tingling sensation running down my spine.

I had questions in my mind throughout the Bible study and service. I listened to the teaching but did not understand everything I heard.

I decided to wait till after the Bible studies and service after the teenagers had gone before asking my grandfather my questions. I asked my grandfather, 'who is this Jesus'? He told me that Jesus died for our sins a long time ago.

He told me Jesus was the only begotten son of God who was born of the virgin Mary and came to this world to die for our sins. Then he quoted a scripture to me:

For God so loved the world that he gave his one and only Son, that whoever believes in him shall not perish but have eternal life.
John 3:16 (NIV)

I did not understand the things he told me about Jesus Christ, but I was able to gather the basic information about Christ dying for my sins.

I asked him more questions about Jesus, and he tried to explain it to me in as simple terms as possible. Then I asked him what my father would say if he knew I loved Jesus. My grandfather said nothing.

He had no answer to that question because of the religious and cultural implications surrounding my falling in love with Jesus. My parents would instantly conclude that he was the one who talked me into accepting Jesus Christ. Even at that age, I had some idea of what rifts such a development could cause between my parents and my grandfather.

Soon it was time for me to return home and to the reality awaiting me. I had enough understanding of the situation. I knew my parents would not want to hear that I participated in a Christian ritual or had an interest in the name Jesus. I left my grandfather's place with a resolution to hold on to my love for Jesus Christ without necessarily letting my parents know. Within me, I knew something had changed forever; I had found a source of joy that no one could take away from me.

You make known to me the path of life;
  you will fill me with joy in your presence,
  with eternal pleasures at your right hand.
Psalms 16:11(NIV)

Life in the United State of America.

Let us fast-forward to December 26th, 1982, when my aunt sponsored us from Guyana, South America, to the United States of America. My parents and three siblings came to the United States, making up five of us. There was a sense of relief in the family when we eventually arrived, knowing we now could have the hope of living a better life: the "American Dream." As should be expected, my parents nursed the nostalgia of leaving their homeland for a while, but we, the children, were too excited about the beauty of our new home to think of whatever we missed back in Guyana.

For a foreigner to work in the United States of America, they must have the necessary credentials, which I did not have at the time. Before enrolling in a college, I had to enroll in a community program to get my grade equivalent diploma test (GED). I did an undergraduate course at New York University and my graduate course at Hunter College, where I bagged a degree in Business Administration.

At college, I worked out like a gym rat. I wanted to be a bodybuilder, so I worked out in the gymnasium daily. I alternated between my studies and my gymnasium activities. My low-level social life helped my interest and commitment to bodybuilding. One day I hurt my back while working out, ending my dream of becoming a bodybuilder.

After graduating from Hunter College, I remained ambitious but still quite naïve. I was determined to take on the world and make something meaningful from the opportunity to live in the United States. At the time, I was still living with my parents. To save the cost of rent and commuting, we lived in the basement of my aunt's house.

After leaving college, I went on several interviews and eventually landed a job. My first job was at Colgate Palmolive Company in New York City. I was pleased to get the job even though it was far from where I lived. At that time, I was living in Queens with my folks. I worked with the company for about thirteen years in the International Far East Division.

Over time the pressure of the job got at me. I got burnt out, getting up early for work and getting home late.

The long-distance going and returning from work began to take a toll on my health. I, however, had no thought of stopping the job at the time, even though I had little time to spend with my family and was always away during the days. I never knew that the stress I was going through would eventually lead to my testimony and a significant encounter with God. Whenever we worked late, we got a company car to take us home, so I was extremely fortunate to have that luxury occasionally. The New York City subways were far from safe late at night, so the provision of being given a ride home was very much welcomed.

My aunt was extremely popular in her community, having stayed there for a long time before I relocated there with my immediate family to stay with her. She had a lot of friends within and without our immediate Guyanese community, and some of her friends were also from Hindu backgrounds. This made them stick close together.

One fateful Saturday morning, one of her Hindu friends invited us to a Hindu wedding. We were excited about the prospect of attending a Hindu wedding, which was not exactly as common as we used to have back home in Guyana.

We attended the wedding and met many people from Hindu backgrounds like us. It was reminiscent of Guyana, except that the setting was better and was sheer luxury compared to what we used to have back home. I had lots of fun, and my aunt introduced some of her friends to me. Later that evening, one of my aunt's friends, whom I had just met at the event, introduced her brother to me. He seemed to be a lovely young man, and we began talking. He had been in the United States for some time and had quite a lot to talk about that I did not know of then.

Several months after the event, I remained in contact with the young man, and our relationship was pleasant to our respective families. With little or no consent from me, my parents arranged a marriage between us through my aunt's friend, my friend's elder sister.

We eventually got married in a moderate Hindu wedding ceremony, and about a year later, we had a wonderful daughter. That year was spent trying to understand each other, or at least I wanted to understand him as best as possible.

It was April 1986, and the weather was cold in New York. We were living in a two-bedroom apartment in Brooklyn.

It was a Friday evening, and I was in the middle of attending to my six-week-old child when her father, my husband, stormed into the bedroom. It was unusual of him, and I was jolted by his attitude that evening. He slapped my face, and I got a nasty cut on my upper lip. He smelled alcohol and cigarettes. He started an ugly quarrel with me and started hitting me again. He proceeded to scatter the whole house, shouting and behaving like someone highly intoxicated.

I was hurt and highly disappointed in him, making him know as much. I realized carrying on a match with him would only result in more damage. I was also not ready to physically retaliate, so I had to switch to an alternative plan.

I called my mom on the phone to inform her of the unfortunate situation in my house. After the call, I picked up my child and a few things I may immediately need. I left the house before he could hold me down and drove to my mom's house. That was the last time I saw his place as I never returned to that apartment after that unfortunate incident that fateful evening.

I recall driving in the darkness of night with so much hurt in my mind. I could feel my lips swollen, and my upper lip was bleeding.

The pain, the disappointment, and the betrayal were so unexpected. I never thought of marrying, only to become a punching bag to my husband. My baby cried through some of the distance, worsening my feeling. It was an image I could not clear from my head for a long time.

His family and mine got involved in the issue between myself and my estranged husband to mediate between us. After a few meetings with back and forth talking, it was obvious my husband was not remorseful, nor was he ready to change. I stood my ground against returning to such an abusive relationship unless he was willing to agree to my terms. Unfortunately, he was not ready. Eventually, I had to divorce him for my peace of mind and that of my baby.

The divorce option was not easy. There were lots of factors coming to play that I had to cope with. Our Hindu culture, the feelings of my family, and his own family too that I had grown to accept as my own family. Not only that, managing a full-time job with a baby who was at the time still noticeably young was a challenge.

I returned to my aunt's house, where my parents were staying. I returned to stay with them in the basement, hoping to gather myself. That event was perhaps the first significant low in my life.

I was, however, determined to cope somehow. Many are the afflictions of the righteous: but the LORD delivereth him out of them all.

The righteous person may have many troubles,

   but the Lord delivers him from them all;

20 he protects all his bones,

   not one of them will be broken.

Palms 34:19-20 (NIV)

Chapter Four

Trying Out a Second Time.

Not so long after, a tenant moved out of my aunt's house. A flat became vacant, so my parents moved from the basement to the third floor to occupy the empty apartment. I moved out of the basement with my parents and stayed with them in the new apartment on the third floor for a while. At the time, it was the wise thing to do. I needed my mom to help care for my little daughter. I was so grateful that I had her around for support.

One day another of my aunt's friends came to visit her. My aunt was in the living room with her friend, and my parents soon joined them. They were in the middle of a cheerful conversation when I happened to walk in. My aunt's friend saw me and was probably attracted to me. She responded to my greetings and other traditional pleasantries and asked if I was single or engaged. As expected, my parents and aunt gave her a summary of that aspect of my story. My aunt's friend looked at me keenly with an expression I could not readily put a description to.

Then she said that her brother-in-law was also single and was looking for a wife at the time.

That was the kind of news my parents loved to hear. They beamed with pleasure at hearing her announcement. I knew my mom was excited at the possibility of seeing me remarry. That was something she wanted to happen as fast as possible, and it appeared her dream was about to happen.

My aunt, on the other hand, was also pleased. She could easily see through the conversation and tell where the matter was going. She knew she wielded much influence in my affair, and it would just be a matter of her giving her consent.

My only problem with the whole issue was how my family held so firmly to our Guyana culture to my detriment. I watched on in silence; I could not tell how exactly I was supposed to feel. I did not know if to feel glad at another chance to try again to find true love and an untroubled home or worry about another lousy outcome. My worries were not considered at the end of the day.

In their old-fashioned ways, my parents agreed with everything my aunt told them to do.

They trusted her absolutely and knew she had influence within the community and total power in her household, of which they were a part. I could not tell if my parents were afraid to say no to her because they were living at her place. This even though they were not staying there for free: they were paying her monthly rent.

For me, I did not have a voice. I had no say in my parent's and aunt's decisions over me. I had to do whatever they told me to do. I was not happy about them deciding my fate. Back home in Guyana, it was a norm, but after spending time in the western world and seeing the modern culture, I was no longer comfortable with others deciding my fate. However, there was little I could do to salvage the situation.

They arranged for this man to come to my aunt's house. I did not know the man and met him that day for the first time. But in the Hindu culture, relations could arrange marriages for prospective couples, and it is something they still do over there today. Like I said earlier, I was not comfortable with the arrangement. I was in such before, and it ended badly; I was not keen to walk into another mess with my eyes open.

I immediately made my displeasure known to my relations. They simply ignored me and continued with the wedding arrangement. When the day drew near, I fought them so hard.

They were surprised at my stance and decided to play a delicate card against me. They were so angry that they told me that if I did not marry the man, the inheritance or dowry would not come to me. I told them I did not care but would not marry a stranger.

When that card failed, they decided to bring the family name into the equation. I was told my disobedience was taboo and would stain the family name. That was hard to navigate, and I had to succumb to their demand. Eventually, I had to marry the man to keep the Singh title intact.

I knew little or nothing about this man, but since I had given my word to my family, I decided to put in more effort to save my marriage. I was concerned about his somewhat secretive attitude and the fact that we had no chemistry. Unlike the case with my first husband, I did not get to talk much with my second husband before the wedding. I knew little about him; marrying him was like walking in the dark and hoping there was no obstacle ahead.

I married for the second time, hoping that we could get things right this time. It was not long before several red flags started flashing. I had resigned to my fate and kept hoping somehow something would happen, and eventually, everything would turn out to be okay. I hoped and hoped to no avail; things only got worse. He began to do some things he did in hiding in the open. His negative attitudes started to come up increasingly by the day.

The second marriage was identical to the first adventure I had. Alcohol and cigarettes were the food of my husband. Initially, he gave the impression that he was willing to make some effort to make things work out between us. Unfortunately, as the years rolled by, he only got worse instead of improving. I felt hurt and let down.

Along the line, I gave birth to another beautiful baby girl. I expected the arrival of our baby to calm my husband down, but that was not to be. I thought he would at least cut down on his alcohol and cigarettes addiction since we had a neonate in the house, but that never happened. After several years of enduring rather than enjoying, I realized I could not go on living the way I was. I arrived at a point when I had to decide for myself and my daughter. It was a familiar situation I had hoped never to experience again.

Unfortunately, it was a case of the same film reeling out before my eyes.

My marriage to my second husband lasted for about fifteen years. After fifteen years, I decided I could not cope anymore. Living with a man who kept to himself and smoked and drank all day was not my idea of marriage. The quarrels, our vast differences in priorities, and views on life, coupled with the smoke from his cigarettes, threatened my health and that of my baby, and I had to leave the marriage.

Even though I had not officially divorced my second husband, I decided to move upstate within New York. I sold my house in Queens and moved out. My priority was to give my kids a better life. I sold my house, left Queens in New York City, and moved about a hundred miles north to New Paltz with my beautiful daughters. I bought a beautiful home there, and I still live in New Paltz to this day. My girls were little, and I wanted at all costs to give them an excellent education by getting them into a top school to attend. The right environment also influenced my decision to move to New Paltz.

After the relocation, I focused on getting a divorce from my unfortunate second marriage. Getting the divorce procedure over was a relief. It all went smoothly and relatively fast. Once I was through with that, I focused on giving my girls the best I could afford.

Getting that divorce was one of the best decisions I have ever made. I will refrain from admitting that the fifteen years spent in the second marriage were a wasted fifteen years. However, it was not the best period of my life. That marriage should not have happened in the first place, but I got a beautiful daughter from it anyway. I recall all my effort to make my relations see why it was not the best for me, but the worst had been done. I felt I had wasted a huge chunk of my life, and the years could no longer be rolled back. However, something deep inside me told me there was nothing too hard for God to do, and He alone could make up for our lost, wasted years.

"I will repay you for the years the locusts have eaten—
the great locust and the young locust,
the other locusts and the locust swarm[a]—
my great army that I sent among you.
26 You will have plenty to eat until you are full,
and you will praise the name of the Lord your God,
who has worked wonders for you;
never again will my people be shamed.
Joel 2:25-26 (NIV)

Chapter Five

The Healing Hands of Jehovah Rahpa.

I began commuting from New Paltz to New York City on the Metro North Train out of the Poughkeepsie Station, spending five hours on the train daily. I went to the gymnasium every night and on weekends to keep in shape. Apart from keeping physically fit, I needed something to put my energy and attention to. It was a helpful distraction that helped me to retain my sanity and helped me relax.

Some months later, I started to feel pain in my back. Initially, I dismissed it as the usual pain from muscle fatigue. After some time, the pain persisted and got even worse. At that point, I knew I needed to seek professional help. I booked appointments with several sports doctors who told me I had two bad intervertebral joints in my lower back, worn-out cartilages and grossly reduced joint spaces. The intervertebral discs had worn out, and the bones were grinding where there was supposed to be padding from the intervertebral discs. I was made to understand that the situation was terrible and that I needed back surgery.

Let us fast-forward to November twenty-nine, 1999. I met Glenn, and we started to date. He had a beautiful farmhouse about five miles from my home that I found attractive. He worked for the Telephone company, was a faithful churchgoer, and was remarkably busy in the Baptist Church.

I told him about my back pain, and Glenn met me in severe pain one day. He told me that the United States Food and Drug Administration agency had developed an IDET, Intra Discal Electrothermal Therapy. It is said to be a minimally invasive procedure but was not approved by the national authority. It is a surgical tool whereby the doctor makes an incision and goes into the back, not unlike laparoscopy. The device is effective enough to go into the back and mend the damage. The surgery never took place as my health insurance did not approve the procedure. Seemingly bad news, but in retrospect, I was to see that this was for the name of God to be glorified.

Then one Friday evening came; I remember that day so well, as I had mentioned much earlier. I got off the Metro North train to go to my car and had the worst pain in my back. I could hardly walk.

When I eventually managed to get to the car, I could not get my left leg in the car. It was such an excruciating pain that I had never experienced. It took the grace of God for me to manage to get into the car and drive home.

The drive home was a horrible experience as my mind stayed on the pain and the cause. I was worried about the extent of damage and the several implications of a surgical correction. Apart from the financial application, I understood that some people had such surgeries on their backs and developed other complications. I was not ready to take a risk that could plunge me into worse, additional pain for the rest of my life.

I struggled to get out of the car on getting home from work, and Glenn came to visit. I told Glenn and my daughters that I was not feeling well and wanted to go to my room. Of course, few people in my life at the time knew about my back pain and were compassionate to me whenever the pain came up as it did that night.

I went to my room, sat on the bed, and then turned on the television in my bedroom. I saw that Pastor Benny Hinn was preaching, and I was suddenly interested. I looked to my right at my nightstand, and there was a Bible.

I picked up the Bible and flipped it open to either the book of Ruth or Esther; I cannot recall which. Even though I still have a clear memory of the momentous events of that fateful night, to this day, I cannot remember which of the two biblical books I opened that night.

I was motivated to read but had no clue what I was reading. Nothing I read made any sense. Then suddenly, I heard Pastor Benny Hinn say on the television, "There is someone sitting with back pain…" That jolted my attention, and I raised my head from the Bible I was reading, focusing my attention on the television screen. The popular, silver-haired televangelist prayed a short healing prayer, which I claimed with an "Amen!"

Suddenly, I felt like two hands held my back from the lumbar area. The hands were hot like fire, and as they did what they had to do on my back, I felt the pain elevate through my back and appeared to be thrown out through my shoulder region. It all happened so fast, with the burning sensation from those two hands lingering in my head for a long time. At that moment, I started to sob and cried so hard. I did not need to be told that something supernatural had happened.

I became so aware of the presence of the Holy Spirit that I got up and gave my life to Jesus Christ.

I knelt in my room and surrendered my life to the King of kings, the Lord of lords, the One who calls the things that be as though they were, the only One with the power to reverse the irreversible. I did not know much about Jesus Christ or Jehovah Rapha then; I would have called Him several beautiful names to appreciate my healing.

After sitting back, I still wanted to be sure that I was genuinely healed, so I knelt again, and I felt like a whole new person; I was as light as a feather. I bent down yet again to make sure that I was healed. After a few twists and turns, I got up with no pain.

He said, "If you listen carefully to the Lord your God and do what is right in his eyes, if you pay attention to his commands and keep all his decrees, I will not bring on you any of the diseases I brought on the Egyptians, for I am the Lord, who heals you."
Exodus 15:26 (NIV)

It was Glenn who first heard me crying. He came into my room, looked at me, and knew something was happening to me. He was sensitive enough not to interrupt whatever supernatural experience I was going through. He stayed a moment longer to be sure I was not crying out of pain, and he then walked out of the room. He waited patiently for me in the living room to return to myself before asking me any questions.

After a while, I regained my composure. Still basking in the euphoria of a supernatural healing experience, I went to the living room to give Glenn and my girls the good news. I announced to them that Jesus had just healed me. I told them that I did not have to take any pain medications prescribed by the sports doctors anymore. They were all amazed. I understand that some skepticism still lingered at the back of their minds, and there was a need to learn all such lingering doubts, but that could wait till later.

I asked Glenn to call his Baptist church pastor to arrange for my water baptism. He put a call across to his pastor, explaining what had just happened and my desire to be baptized after giving my life to Jesus. The pastor obliged happily, and an arrangement was made to that effect.

I was baptized the following week and invited all my Hindu family members to witness the event.

A few days afterward, I went back to my sports doctor to give him the good news that I did not need surgery anymore, that Jesus had healed me. I walked into his office with no sign of pain or distress. He was very skeptical of my report and requested an X-ray of my back. He marveled and was surprised that my back discs were straight and knit back in place like a baby's disc. He was amazed at the miracle. It was also double proof for me too that Jesus healed me. That was my first significant healing encounter with Jesus.

Heal me, Lord, and I will be healed;
   save me and I will be saved,
   for you are the one I praise.
Jeremiah 17: 14 (NIV)

Sharing my Testimony with the World.

I continued to do the long commute to and from New York City to New Paltz on the Metro North train. The long hours of sitting were still boring, but mercifully the pain in my back had gone without any residual effect. I was aware of the difference in my life and could not thank God enough for the experience. I continued my little efforts to know more about Jesus Christ.

Then one evening, I received an invitation from Joyce Meyer Ministries. It came as a surprise but one that was welcomed. She was coming to the Pepsi Arena in Albany, New York, and wanted to know if I would like to assist in ushering at the event. I was so excited that I replied yes without a second thought.

I excitedly waited for the event through the days that appeared to slow down towards the days of the event. The day finally came, and I made myself available to serve. I ushered for three days, and I thoroughly enjoyed the experience.

On the second day of the explosive event, the marketing team approached me and asked if I would do a video about my journey with Jesus. I thought it was an excellent opportunity to let the world know what the Lord has done in my life. I accepted the offer, which eventually led to this book's writing. I can honestly say that this book was birthed by my answer to one invitation through email to serve. That singular acceptance of the opportunity to serve in a Christian program led to the next stage of my journey with Jesus.

The media team of Joyce Meyer ministries filmed my story, and it was shown around the world. Joyce Meyer herself was also featured in the documentary. It was a significant high in my journey as a follower of Jesus Christ. There were people who knew me and were surprised to see me on the air in a documentary about my journey with Jesus. I must confess that the documentary was a boost to my faith in Jesus.

The thought of my testimony drawing people to Jesus was another important part of that wonderful experience. It is refreshing and nostalgic that God had singled me out for such an encounter and used me to touch many lives.

The documentary was a summer of my Christian experience. It started by briefly mentioning my Hindu background, how I first learned about Jesus, and my experience with Him from there on.

As expected, the climax of the documentary was my miraculous healing. My clinical test results were compared before and after the healing, and the few witnesses to the incredible miracle were also involved.

Afterward, I felt like a star as the flood light was on me all through. Several people wanted to meet me, and some asked questions about my testimony. From that point on, I knew there was no going back. I knew the next thing I could do was find my purpose in Christ Jesus.

Not long after, I decided I needed a career path change. After some days of consideration, I opted for the banking world. Eventually, I got a job with a stock broking firm instead. I had nursed the idea of working in such a setting for some time as I found the nature of what they do fascinating.

Working in the sector was entirely different from what I was used to.

The trading floor was like the belly of a colossal beast where activities go on non-stop in a rollercoaster fashion.

The trading floors host both International and domestic stock trading. The noise that emanated from the trading activities was like that of a betting arena. The name of the stockbroker firm I worked with was JP Morgan, and I worked with them for some years before I had to consider a change of job again.

After six years of working with JP Morgan, the unbelievable happened. That was the year of the World Trade Center explosion. I saw the two planes fly towards the second tower through my office window. I first thought it was a television media helicopter. Then moments later, the aircraft disappeared into the tower, and black smoke emerged from the tower. I knew at that point it was a terrorist attack. The thought of a terrorist attack of that magnitude in the city of New York was not only unsettling but also unlikely. I felt such a city's security and intelligence mechanisms should be sound enough to detect such attacks well ahead of time. Although when the news of how the attack happened broke, I better understood the unfortunate event.

However, getting the complete information or not, my mind was already made up. That was the day I decided to quit my job with JP Morgan in the ever-busy city of New York. I decided to seek local employment at a location closer to my home.

Even though I expected to find more options for jobs in the sprawling working system that the city of New York has become, I still trusted God to help me with alternative employment elsewhere. I cannot forget the relief on my daughters when they confirmed that I was not affected by the now famous 9/11 attack. I did not want to risk my life or the peace of my loved ones hence the decision to quit my job. While searching for a new job, I decided to take a few days off to rest my nerves.

In their hearts, humans plan their course,
  but the Lord establishes their steps.
Proverbs 16:9 (NIV)

Chapter Seven

A Wonderful Family of Christ.

*L*et us fast-forward to 2019 and how Princess Belemzy Ministries (PBM) and School of Power (SOP) changed my life. I came to Apostle Queen Belema Abili (Apostle) through someone I would now instead refer to as a false prophet. I listened to him on social media but was never led to do any assignments from the false prophet. However, he did not give out assignments to his followers on social media, except for occasional fasting. He was very charismatic but also very controlling.

Sometime in 2019, I had a dream about Apostle. I saw her in a big stadium in a white dress. She was with her cousin and the false one. I was in the audience, in a row close to the front. Like a few others, I moved closer to her and stretched my hands out to get a touch from her. I never knew it was a revelation of what would come in the distant future.

The first time I saw Apostle, I immediately fell in love with her; her appearance, demeanor, and amiable way of bringing people close to her appealed to me. She also has some funny sayings like "Chai" and "Abeg," which are expressions in pidgin English spoken in the western part of Africa. I suppose that suggests her root.

I connected with her, but I still did not understand the Bible. I would listen and listen to her sermons. When she cried, I would cry. I would ask God to help her. I kept on listening to her 24/7. I was never tired of her voice or message, even though there were many things she would say that I struggled to understand.

Fast-forward to April 24[th,] 2020, and I got a new job. I woke up that morning to shower and get ready for work. Apostle was on the air, and God spoke through her. The television was tuned to the channel where her programs get aired often.

Suddenly, I heard her say: "I will send someone else if you don't do what I asked you to do." I broke down and began to cry out to God. Please, God, send her. I took some time to pray before returning to my daily activities.

Her ministry has changed my life. I have grown to love God more than ever because of her ministerial activities. I still cry a lot when I hear the name Jesus. The Holy Spirit put that feeling in my heart for me to love everyone. I do not know if I have any enemies out there. Sometimes I feel I do not have any families or friends anywhere in the world. My only friend and confidant is Jesus.

As I grew in my knowledge of Jesus through PBM-SOP, I could focus more. I could fast with no challenges; even when challenges arise, despite them, I can still complete the fasting.

Aside from learning the word of God and the ways of a true Christian, there were other things I learned through Apostle's ministry. The ministry organizes vocational seminars and other empowerment programs from which I also learned a thing or two.

For instance, the ministry taught me how to make juices of diverse types. Apostle shared everything she knew with us. She did not hide anything from us and was concerned for our growth spiritually and otherwise. She lived her life with her followers like an open book that anyone could read through. She is a wonderful child of God.

Her ministry is God's ministry, and there is no contesting that. Evidence shows how the ministry has touched so many lives within and without the United States of America. God has given us the best through His daughter, Apostle, and He expects the best from us.

PBM-SOP has been a source of comfort to many who came mourning, the lonely, the hopeless, and those whose loved ones had given up on them. God has used Apostle to restore the life of many of these people, giving them joy for sadness and excitement in place of the heaviness of heart. He has given us beauty for ashes through Apostle according to His word.

and provide for those who grieve in Zion—
to bestow on them a crown of beauty
   instead of ashes,
the oil of joy
   instead of mourning,
and a garment of praise
   instead of a spirit of despair.
They will be called oaks of righteousness,
   a planting of the Lord
   for the display of his splendor.
Isaiah 61:3 (NIV)

There was something Apostle said in one of her videos, and those words still ring in my head today. She said God likes it when we come to Him knowing nothing so He can teach us everything. I am humbled, to say the least. I am so humbled to learn from and respect the Holy Spirit.

I learned a lot of lessons in virtue from PBM-SOP; it taught me how to be selfless. I understood that when God gives us an assignment, we are expected to do it and not quench the fire of the Holy Spirit.

There are no shortcuts with God. That is yet another principle I learned. As a child of God, instructions should be followed to the letter. Trying to run ahead of the message can only lead to disaster.

PBM-SOP has taught me how to obey and respect my fellow students in the quest for the knowledge of God.

I keep telling the Lord Jesus Christ, "Don't cast me away and never take your Holy Spirit from me." My daily hunger and longing were to know Him more.

What is more, I consider everything a loss because of the surpassing worth of knowing Christ Jesus my Lord, for whose sake I have lost all things. I consider them garbage, that I may gain Christ

9 and be found in him, not having a righteousness of my own that comes from the law, but that which is through faith in[a] Christ—the righteousness that comes from God on the basis of faith.

10 I want to know Christ—yes, to know the power of his resurrection and participation in his sufferings, becoming like him in his death

Philippians 3:8-10 (NIV)

One day while Apostle was amid a fast that she encouraged her followers to join, I got a peculiar assignment. It was a seven-day assignment to write about taking my Hindu family out of bondage. I had previously vowed to always obey the Holy Spirit, so when the inspiration came, I obeyed Him without delay because I trusted Him to perfect whatever He was leading me to do in His name.

But Samuel replied:

"Does the Lord delight in burnt offerings and sacrifices
　as much as in obeying the Lord?
To obey is better than sacrifice,
　and to heed is better than the fat of rams.
1 Samuel 15: 22 (NIV)

Chapter Eight

Liberating my Loving Family from Bondage.

HEAVENLY ASSIGNMENT

Day 1

God says: "Look at what is happening to the people in India. They are kicking their gods in the streets because their gods are not healing them from Covid-19." God says He is separating the grain from the chaff.

His winnowing fork is in his hand, and he will clear his threshing floor, gathering his wheat into the barn and burning up the chaff with unquenchable fire."
Matthew 3:12 (NIV)

He is ready to separate the chaff from the wheat with His

winnowing fork.

Then He will clean up the threshing area, gathering the wheat into his barn but burning the chaff with never-ending fire.

After I obeyed and posted Day 1 assignment God gave me about my Hindu family, He says Do Not Fear, For I Am With You. Hallelujah

So do not fear, for I am with you;
　do not be dismayed, for I am your God.
I will strengthen you and help you;
　I will uphold you with my righteous right hand.
Isaiah 41:10 (NIV)

Day 2

He was bringing my Hindu families out of bondage! When you give your life to Christ, He gives you a new, regenerated heart. He turns your heart of stone into a heart of flesh. He shows you how to stop living for yourself and start serving others.

There is no doubt that you have some people you love heading to hell. With this in mind, we should intercede daily for them that Christ would draw them out of the muck and mire; and set their feet on a solid foundation in Himself. There is only one way to salvation and eternal life of joy. That only way is Jesus Christ.

Jesus saith unto him, I am the way, the truth, and the life: no man cometh unto the Father, but by me.
John 14:6 (KJV)

For those receptive to your faith, you can do some serious seed planting by showing them verses from the Bible to help them decide to follow Christ. After this step, you prayerfully follow up with them until they are walking in the ways of Jesus Christ.

But God demonstrates his love for us in this: While we were still sinners, Christ died for us.
Romans 5:8 (NIV)

This is love: not that we loved God, but that he loved us and sent his Son as an atoning sacrifice for our sins.
1 John 4:10 (NIV)

Day 3

But Esau ran to meet Jacob and embraced him; he threw his arms around his neck and kissed him. And they wept.
Genesis 33:4 (NIV)

11 Jesus continued: "There was a man who had two sons. 12 The younger one said to his father, 'Father, give me my share of the estate.' So he divided his property between them.

13 "Not long after that, the younger son got together all he had, set off for a distant country and there squandered his wealth in wild living.

14 After he had spent everything, there was a severe famine in that whole country, and he began to be in need.

15 So he went and hired himself out to a citizen of that country, who sent him to his fields to feed pigs.

16 He longed to fill his stomach with the pods that the pigs were eating, but no one gave him anything.

17 "When he came to his senses, he said, 'How many of my father's hired servants have food to spare, and here I am starving to death!

18 I will set out and go back to my father and say to him: Father, I have sinned against heaven and against you.

19 I am no longer worthy to be called your son; make me like one of your hired servants.'

20 So he got up and went to his father.

"But while he was still a long way off, his father saw him and was filled with compassion for him; he ran to his son, threw his arms around him and kissed him.

21 "The son said to him, 'Father, I have sinned against heaven and against you. I am no longer worthy to be called your son.'

22 "But the father said to his servants, 'Quick! Bring the best robe and put it on him. Put a ring on his finger and sandals on his feet.

23 Bring the fattened calf and kill it. Let's have a feast and celebrate.

24 For this son of mine was dead and is alive again; he was lost and is found.' So they began to celebrate.

Luke 15:1-22 (NIV)

Just like the prodigal son became broken and repentant, so Jacob did. As the living father forgives, embraces, and wept with the son, so Esau did with his brother Jacob.

It is a beautiful picture of forgiveness. Forgiveness begins with an encounter with God as the originator of forgiveness. He is the one with the limitless capacity to forgive.

His forgiveness engulfs us with a capacity, a mandate, and a reservoir of forgiveness. Because God has thoroughly forgiven us through Christ, we can and must forgive others for Christ's sake. Forgiveness is the essence of being a Christian. Without the grace to forgive others who wrong us, we cannot lay claim to being true Christians and forgive ourselves. Forgiveness is a fundamental part of Christianity.

Pray to turn your life around and become a Christian. Forgive, say the salvation prayer as seen in this book, and accept Jesus as your Lord and personal Savior. Amen!

Day 4

My Hindu families are in slavery, and I use this scripture to free them from their gods; hallelujah! Paul used the word "slavery" many times in Galatians, including Galatians 5:

It is for freedom that Christ has set us free. Stand firm, then, and do not let yourselves be burdened again by a yoke of slavery.
Galatians 5:1 (NIV)

Earlier in Galatians, Paul spoke of an incident where some people had tried to get him and other ministers to require gentile males to be circumcised. Regarding this situation, Paul wrote:

This matter arose because some false believers had infiltrated our ranks to spy on the freedom we have in Christ Jesus and to make us slaves.
Galatians 2:4 (NIV)

WHAT IS SLAVERY?

Slavery implies bondage or slavish thinking. As many do, a cursory reading of these passages might lead you to assume that Paul considered commandment-keeping as bondage.

Slavery is anything that puts you under the authority of the devil. When you allow sin to draw you away from the umbrella of salvation in Christ Jesus, you find yourself in the darkness of the devil's bondage. It is therefore not biblical to refer to any law by God as bondage.

Now the Lord is the Spirit, and where the Spirit of the Lord is, there

is freedom.
2 Corinthians 3:17 (NIV)

Day 5

My Hindu families are in bondage from worshiping their false gods. In the Hindu religion, they worship thousands of different gods.

Therefore, bringing them out of the worship of the several false gods will push back the spirit of bondage over them and will free them. No god can deliver from bondage but the only true God.

Three Hebrew boys demonstrated as much in the book of Daniel chapter three when they withstood the powerful king Nebuchadnezzar and his god.

King Nebuchadnezzar made an image of gold, sixty cubits high and six cubits wide,[a] and set it up on the plain of Dura in the province of Babylon.

2 He then summoned the satraps, prefects, governors, advisers, treasurers, judges, magistrates and all the other provincial officials to come to the dedication of the image he had set up.

3 So the satraps, prefects, governors, advisers, treasurers, judges, magistrates and all the other provincial officials assembled for the dedication of the image that King Nebuchadnezzar had set up, and they stood before it.

4 Then the herald loudly proclaimed, "Nations and peoples of every language, this is what you are commanded to do:

5 As soon as you hear the sound of the horn, flute, zither, lyre, harp, pipe and all kinds of music, you must fall down and worship the image of gold that King Nebuchadnezzar has set up.

6 Whoever does not fall down and worship will immediately be thrown into a blazing furnace."

7 Therefore, as soon as they heard the sound of the horn, flute, zither, lyre, harp and all kinds of music, all the nations and peoples of every language fell down and worshiped the image of gold that King Nebuchadnezzar had set up.

8 At this time some astrologers[b] came forward and denounced the Jews.

9 They said to King Nebuchadnezzar, "May the king live forever!

10 Your Majesty has issued a decree that everyone who hears the sound of the horn, flute, zither, lyre, harp, pipe and all kinds of music must fall down and worship the image of gold,

11 and that whoever does not fall down and worship will be thrown into a blazing furnace.

12 But there are some Jews whom you have set over the affairs of the province of Babylon—Shadrach, Meshach and Abednego—who pay no attention to you, Your Majesty. They neither serve your gods nor worship

the image of gold you have set up."

13 Furious with rage, Nebuchadnezzar summoned Shadrach, Meshach and Abednego. So these men were brought before the king,

14 and Nebuchadnezzar said to them, "Is it true, Shadrach, Meshach and Abednego, that you do not serve my gods or worship the image of gold I have set up?

15 Now when you hear the sound of the horn, flute, zither, lyre, harp, pipe and all kinds of music, if you are ready to fall down and worship the image I made, very good. But if you do not worship it, you will be thrown immediately into a blazing furnace. Then what god will be able to rescue you from my hand?"

16 Shadrach, Meshach and Abednego replied to him, "King Nebuchadnezzar, we do not need to defend ourselves before you in this matter.

17 If we are thrown into the blazing furnace, the God we serve is able to deliver us from it, and he will deliver us[c] from Your Majesty's hand.

18 But even if he does not, we want you to know, Your Majesty, that we will not serve your gods or worship the image of gold you have set up."

19 Then Nebuchadnezzar was furious with Shadrach, Meshach and Abednego, and his attitude toward them changed. He ordered the furnace heated seven times hotter than usual

20 and commanded some of the strongest soldiers in his army to tie up Shadrach, Meshach and Abednego and throw them into the blazing furnace.

21 So these men, wearing their robes, trousers, turbans and other clothes, were bound and thrown into the blazing furnace.

22 The king's command was so urgent and the furnace so hot that the flames of the fire killed the soldiers who took up Shadrach, Meshach and Abednego,

23 and these three men, firmly tied, fell into the blazing furnace.

24 Then King Nebuchadnezzar leaped to his feet in amazement and asked his advisers, "Weren't there three men that we tied up and threw into the fire?"

They replied, "Certainly, Your Majesty."

25 He said, "Look! I see four men walking around in the fire, unbound and unharmed, and the fourth looks like a son of the gods."

26 Nebuchadnezzar then approached the opening of the blazing furnace and shouted, "Shadrach, Meshach and Abednego, servants of the Most High God, come out! Come here!"

So Shadrach, Meshach and Abednego came out of the fire,

27 and the satraps, prefects, governors and royal advisers crowded around them. They saw that the fire had not harmed their bodies, nor was a hair

of their heads singed; their robes were not scorched, and there was no smell of fire on them.

28 Then Nebuchadnezzar said, "Praise be to the God of Shadrach, Meshach and Abednego, who has sent his angel and rescued his servants! They trusted in him and defied the king's command and were willing to give up their lives rather than serve or worship any god except their own God.

29 Therefore I decree that the people of any nation or language who say anything against the God of Shadrach, Meshach and Abednego be cut into pieces and their houses be turned into piles of rubble, for no other god can save in this way."

30 Then the king promoted Shadrach, Meshach and Abednego in the province of Babylon.

Daniel 3:1-30 (NIV)

The God of heaven showed up for them and delivered them. Therefore, I trust God for my total deliverance and my family.

Escape The House of Bondage

And it will be like a sign on your hand and a symbol on your forehead that the Lord brought us out of Egypt with his mighty hand."
Exodus 13:16 (NIV)

For generations, the Israelites had suffered cruel oppression, but that was about to change suddenly and dramatically, as God promised Moses:

Moreover, I have heard the groaning of the Israelites, whom the Egyptians are enslaving, and I have remembered my covenant.

6 "Therefore, say to the Israelites: 'I am the Lord, and I will bring you out from under the yoke of the Egyptians. I will free you from being slaves to them, and I will redeem you with an outstretched arm and with mighty acts of judgment.

7 I will take you as my own people, and I will be your God. Then you will know that I am the Lord your God, who brought you out from under the yoke of the Egyptians.

8 And I will bring you to the land I swore with uplifted hand to give to Abraham, to Isaac and to Jacob. I will give it to you as a possession. I am the Lord.'"

Exodus 6:5-8 (NIV)

Perhaps, these great promises also apply to your life today. As you await your breakthrough, maybe you need God to bring you OUT from under your burdens, to rescue you from some kind of bondage, to show you His Supernatural redemption, and to bring you into your spiritual inheritance. That is precisely what He wants to do for you! And never forget that during the first Passover feast, the Israelites were not just released from slavery, as wonderful as that was:

The Israelites did as Moses instructed and asked the Egyptians for articles of silver and gold and for clothing.

36 The Lord had made the Egyptians favorably disposed toward the people, and they gave them what they asked for; so they plundered the Egyptians.

Exodus 12:35-36 (NIV)

The Lord caused the Egyptians to look favorably on the Israelites, and they gave the Israelites whatever they asked for. So they stripped the Egyptians of their wealth!

There can never be a void in the spiritual realm. An entity is filled with an evil spirit or the Holy Spirit. Additionally, man is either of Christ or the devil, blessed or cursed. There is no sitting on the fence regarding sensitive spiritual matters.

God knows this principle, which was why as the children of Israel were leaving the land of Egypt where they were held captive, God arranged for them to be blessed.

The Bible says:

When the Lord takes pleasure in anyone's way,
 He causes their enemies to make peace with them.
Proverbs 16:7 (NIV)

Because the ways of the children of Israel pleased the Lord, He compelled the Egyptians, their enemies, to be at peace with them. Not only that, He made them willingly part with their valuables so that the children of Israel might be blessed. God can consistently deliver from bondage and replace a curse with a blessing or sadness with joy.

Day 6

A Hindu from a vegetarian community often encounters a challenge in a change of dietary customs. When joining the Christian community, diet is one of the sharp contrasts between what used to be and what is. The difference in diet often isolates them from their family, who are still in the Hindu practice.

As much as possible, we should remove every obstacle and stumbling block that prevents the caste Hindu from coming to Christ.

But food does not bring us near to God; we are no worse if we do not eat, and no better if we do.

9 Be careful, however, that the exercise of your rights does not become a stumbling block to the weak.

10 For if someone with a weak conscience sees you, with all your knowledge, eating in an idol's temple, won't that person be emboldened to eat what is sacrificed to idols?

11 So this weak brother or sister, for whom Christ died, is destroyed by your knowledge.

1 Corinthians 8:8-11 (NIV)

Therefore, if what I eat causes my brother or sister to fall into sin, I will never eat meat again, so that I will not cause them to fall.

1 Corinthians 8:13 (NIV)

Being a vegetarian or accepting the liberty that God has given you does not make one better than the other. Just as eating meat or not has no direct bearing on your level of knowing Jesus, so does the issue of being a vegetarian or not have a direct effect on your Christianity. We should let the cross of Christ become the only obstacle for the Hindu, not social issues.

Therefore let us stop passing judgment on one another. Instead, make up your mind not to put any stumbling block or obstacle in the way of a brother or sister.
Romans 14:13 (NIV)

We need to emphasize to the caste Hindus not to leave their community but stay as an obedient believer in Christ within their family and caste community to lead their family and community to Christ.

We have New Testament examples where believers stayed in their community, and we can use scripture to encourage our Hindu friends. The Bible teaches the believer not to be unequally yoked, i.e., for a believer to marry an unbeliever. That does not mean that the Hindu believer must marry outside their community. When the Hindu believer marries another believer from within their caste community, they have a much easier time remaining as salt and light to their community.

God cared about the demon-possessed man from Gerasenes and, through him, saved his entire family:

They went across the lake to the region of the Gerasenes. [a] 2 When Jesus got out of the boat, a man with an impure spirit came from the tombs to meet him.

3 This man lived in the tombs, and no one could bind him anymore, not even with a chain.

4 For he had often been chained hand and foot, but he tore the chains apart and broke the irons on his feet. No one was strong enough to subdue him.

5 Night and day among the tombs and in the hills he would cry out and cut himself with stones.

6 When he saw Jesus from a distance, he ran and fell on his knees in front of him.

7 He shouted at the top of his voice, "What do you want with me, Jesus, Son of the Most High God? In God's name don't torture me!"

8 For Jesus had said to him, "Come out of this man, you impure spirit!"

9 Then Jesus asked him, "What is your name?"

"My name is Legion," he replied, "for we are many."

10 And he begged Jesus again and again not to send them out of the area.

11 A large herd of pigs was feeding on the nearby hillside. 12 The demons begged Jesus, "Send us among the pigs; allow us to go into them."

The demons begged Jesus, "Send us among the pigs; allow us to go into *them."*

13 He gave them permission, and the impure spirits came out and went into the pigs. The herd, about two thousand in number, rushed down the steep bank into the lake and were drowned.

14 Those tending the pigs ran off and reported this in the town and countryside, and the people went out to see what had happened.

When they came to Jesus, they saw the man who had been possessed by the legion of demons, sitting there, dressed and in his right mind; and they were afraid.

16 Those who had seen it told the people what had happened to the demon-possessed man—and told about the pigs as well.

17 Then the people began to plead with Jesus to leave their region.

18 As Jesus was getting into the boat, the man who had been demon-possessed begged to go with him.

19 Jesus did not let him, but said, "Go home to your own people and tell them how much the Lord has done for you, and how he has had mercy on you."

20 So the man went away and began to tell in the Decapolis[a] how much Jesus had done for him. And all the people were amazed.

Mark 5:1-20 (NIV)

When the evil spirits of this demon-possessed man left him, he begged to follow Jesus, but Jesus wanted him to go home and tell his entire family about the gospel. In this way, the family would have the witness of Christ.

When Roman army officer Cornelius came to faith, he did not come out of his family and community and live as the Hebraic Christians; Cornelius remained in his social network, and his entire household was saved through him.

The next day Peter started out with them, and some of the believers from Joppa went along.

24 The following day he arrived in Caesarea. Cornelius was expecting them and had called together his relatives and close friends.

25 As Peter entered the house, Cornelius met him and fell at his feet in reverence.

Acts 10:23-25 (NIV)

Cornelius had invited all his relatives and close friends when Peter came to his home to speak of Christ.

"It is my judgment, therefore, that we should not make it difficult for the Gentiles who are turning to God.
Acts15:19 (NIV)

Day 7

ASSIGNMENT COMPLETED

My Hindu family was in bondage, and the scripture to free them from their gods is taken from Psalm 84. Hallelujah!

How lovely is your dwelling place,
　　Lord Almighty!

2 My soul yearns, even faints,
　　for the courts of the Lord;

my heart and my flesh cry out
　　for the living God.

3 Even the sparrow has found a home,
　　and the swallow a nest for herself,
　　where she may have her young—
a place near your altar,
　　Lord Almighty, my King and my God.

4 Blessed are those who dwell in your house;
　　they are ever praising you.[c]

5 Blessed are those whose strength is in you,
　　whose hearts are set on pilgrimage.

6 As they pass through the Valley of Baka,
　　they make it a place of springs;

    the autumn rains also cover it with pools.[d]

7 They go from strength to strength,
    till each appears before God in Zion.

8 Hear my prayer, Lord God Almighty;
    listen to me, God of Jacob.

9 Look on our shield,[e] O God;
    look with favor on your anointed one.

10 Better is one day in your courts
    than a thousand elsewhere;
I would rather be a doorkeeper in the house of my God
    than dwell in the tents of the wicked.

11 For the Lord God is a sun and shield;
    the Lord bestows favor and honor;
no good thing does he withhold
    from those whose walk is blameless.

12 Lord Almighty,
    blessed is the one who trusts in you.

Psalms 84:1-12 (NIV)

The Valley of Baka is mentioned in Psalms 84, composed by David. He likely wrote this specific psalm when he was exiled from Jerusalem.

This psalm describes the blessedness of relying on God's strength and joy during hardship (vs. 5-8).

It also tells of the longing to be with God daily in His Sanctuary and the blessings there (vs. 1–4, 9–11).

The meaning of the word "Baka…."

The Hebrew word "Baka" relates to bakah, which means "to weep." There are two early versions of the scriptures that shed light on the deep meaning of this phrase. One is known as The LXX and the other as The Vulgate. The LXX is an abbreviation for the Septuagint, the earliest existing Greek translation of the Old Testament from the original Hebrew. In contrast, The Vulgate is the principal Latin version of the Bible, prepared by St. Jerome in the late fourth century and adopted as the official text of the Roman Catholic Church. Both of these respected texts translate the phrase "valley of Baka" as "valley of tears." Elsewhere "Baka" is translated as "mulberry tree."

It is important to note that different translations of The Bible yield different literal content; to show a perfect example with which to drive this point home, behold:

So David inquired of the Lord, but He said, "You shall not go directly up; circle around behind them and come at them in front of the baka-shrubs. **2 Samuel 5:23 (NASB)**

And when David enquired of the Lord, he said, Thou shalt not go up;

but fetch a compass behind them, and come upon them over against the mulberry trees.
2 Samuel 5:23 (KJV)

A mulberry tree is known as a weeping tree, but also one that brings forth mulberries, a delicious fruit. The Valley of Baka was likely a literal place located near Jerusalem.

It may have been the valley of Rephaim:

The Philistines also came and spread themselves in the valley of Rephaim.
2 Samuel 5:18 (NIV)

Perhaps it may also be the Valley of Achor:

And Joshua, and all Israel with him, took Achan the son of Zerah, and the silver, and the garment, and the wedge of gold, and his sons, and his daughters, and his oxen, and his asses, and his sheep, and his tent, and all that he had: and they brought them unto the valley of Achor.
Joshua 7:24 (NIV)

The exact location is unknown; however, it was a valley or a low point in the terrain. Thus, the valley of Baka was a low point of tears or weeping that can bring forth good fruit.

SINNER'S PRAYER

Dear Lord Jesus-

I know I am a sinner, and I ask for Your forgiveness. I believe that You died for my sins and rose from the dead. I turn from my sins and invite You to come into my heart and life. I want to trust and follow You as my Lord and Savior.

Amen!

But God demonstrates his own love for us in this: While we were still sinners, Christ died for us.
Romans 5:8 (NIV)

Forever, continue to obey the voice of God…

Shalom

Chapter Nine

It is a Free Gift for all.

For the grace of God has appeared that offers salvation to all people.

12 It teaches us to say "No" to ungodliness and worldly passions, and to live self-controlled, upright and godly lives in this present age,

13 while we wait for the blessed hope—the appearing of the glory of our great God and Savior, Jesus Christ,

14 who gave himself for us to redeem us from all wickedness and to purify for himself a people that are his very own, eager to do what is good.

Titus 2:11-14 (NIV)

In the beginning, God created man to rule and have dominion over all other creatures.

God blessed them and said to them, "Be fruitful and increase in number; fill the earth and subdue it. Rule over the fish in the sea and the birds in the sky and over every living creature that moves on the ground."
Genesis 1:28 (NIV)

Unfortunately, man fell from the height which God had placed him through the cunningness of Satan. Satan fooled Eve and made her lure Adam into the error of going against the commandment of God.

Since the fall of man in the Garden of Eden, going back to that height of grace has become an impossible goal. The offspring of Adam and Eve over the years have borne the curses incurred by the first two humans due to their error in the Garden of Eden. No wonder the book of Lamentations says:

Our ancestors sinned and are no more,
  and we bear their punishment.
Lamentations 5:7 (NIV)

Even though this text does not directly refer to the fall in the Garden of Eden, the relationship is striking. The Bible makes it clear that man's sins and errors only increased over time. It got to a point when God regretted His investment in man.

The Lord regretted that he had made human beings on the earth, and his heart was deeply troubled.
Genesis 6:6 (NIV)

As a result, God decided to destroy the world except for one man and his family. God decided to start a new world through this single man and his family. It was not only humans that God chose to wipe out. He destroyed animals as well. God instructed the man to gather animals in twos of opposite sexes into a giant ark that He helped the man to build. The man who found favor in the right of God was Noah.

So the Lord said, "I will wipe from the face of the earth the human race I have created—and with them the animals, the birds and the creatures that move along the ground—for I regret that I have made them."
8 But Noah found favor in the eyes of the Lord.
Genesis 6:7-8 (NIV)

Alone, Noah found grace in the eyes of the LORD as expected; however, the seed of evil still passed from the wiped-out race to the new race of men that started through Noah. The same cycle of struggle against sin continued until the first coming of Jesus Christ.

Before the coming of Christ, the Spirit of God only operated through individuals. In other words, grace was not freely accessible to all in general; God used a priest or a few prophets per generation to communicate with His people.

Even though throughout some eras, all seemed well, there was still a need for a mechanism, an avenue through which the entire world could access God without having to go through a single person.

It is of great interest to know that before the coming of Christ, no prophet or individual could mediate between God and his children for a few hundred years. For all those years, none could access the holy presence of the loving God, whose presence is like a burning fire. No man could fulfill the required criteria.

Who may ascend the mountain of the Lord?
  Who may stand in his holy place?
4 The one who has clean hands and a pure heart,
  who does not trust in an idol
  or swear by a false god. [a]
5 They will receive blessing from the Lord
  and vindication from God their Savior.
Psalms 24:3-5 (NIV)

Because there could not be a remission of sin without the shedding of blood, someone had to die to take away the sin of the world. There must be a sacrificial lamb that would pave the way for free entry into the presence of God. However, it was not to be just anybody as specific terms and conditions must be fulfilled.

The individual must be faultless and without sin. He must point men to the way to the Father and then die a painful death on a tree in the form of a crucifix. These three conditions posed another set of challenges as no man could technically fulfill them. To this day, every person is born through sin and inherits sin, therefore failing at the very first hurdle at the moment of conception.

Surely I was sinful at birth,
   sinful from the time my mother conceived me.
Psalms 51:5 (NIV)

Like a man of God once said, every man is born passing between feces and urine; therefore, none could lay claim to perfection; the same mode of delivery of a child hint at the inherent imperfection in every person.

Additionally, the second hurdle was impossible for any man to fulfill. To point the way to God, you must first know that way. Nobody has the requisite knowledge of God to show the entire world the way to God the father before the coming of Christ.

God wanted the whole earth to be flooded with the news of the knowledge of His glory; a condition none could handle, unfortunately.

Prophet Habakkuk prophesied about it a long time ago, yet the fulfillment tarried for hundreds of years:

For the earth will be filled with the knowledge of the glory of the Lord as the waters cover the sea.
Habakkuk 2:14 (NIV)

It does not end there either… there is more bad news…

It is easy for anybody to see why the third hurdle too remained insurmountable for any man. Man naturally does not like pain, nor does he like to suffer for the wrong of another. A natural man will give anything to avoid pain and to stay alive. Even Satan knew as much, and he told God that in the case of Job.

No man was ready to die for the wrong of another. As a result, the gap between God and man remained for thousands of years. Millions of men were born, and they died without ever having an encounter with God. It was a dark period in the history of man.

"Skin for skin!" Satan replied. "A man will give all he has for his own life.
Job 2:4 (NIV)

Very rarely will anyone die for a righteous person, though for a good person someone might possibly dare to die.

8 But God demonstrates his own love for us in this: While we were still sinners, Christ died for us.

Romans 5:7-8 (NIV)

Greater love has no one than this: to lay down one's life for one's friends.
John 15:13 (NIV)

To make matters worse, just as the Israelites turned to idol worship when Moses tarried on the mountain, resulting in the death of many, the same still repeated itself.

When the people saw that Moses was so long in coming down from the mountain, they gathered around Aaron and said, "Come, make us gods[a] who will go before us. As for this fellow Moses who brought us up out of Egypt, we don't know what has happened to him."

2 Aaron answered them, "Take off the gold earrings that your wives, your sons and your daughters are wearing, and bring them to me."

3 So all the people took off their earrings and brought them to Aaron.

4 He took what they handed him and made it into an idol cast in the shape of a calf, fashioning it with a tool. Then they said, "These are your gods, [b] Israel, who brought you up out of Egypt."
Exodus 32:1-4 (NIV)

It is easy to see that humans could no longer hear from God.

When man could no longer hear from God rather than seek Him with diligence, they worsened their predicament by seeking alternative, false gods that could not save them. The result is that they added sin to their sins and a new curse upon their generations going forward.

"Woe to the obstinate children,"
    declares the Lord,

"to those who carry out plans that are not mine,
    forming an alliance, but not by my Spirit,

heaping sin upon sin;

*2 who go down to Egypt
without consulting me;*

*who look for help to Pharaoh's protection,
to Egypt's shade for refuge.*

*3 But Pharaoh's protection will be to your shame,
Egypt's shade will bring you disgrace.*

Isaiah 30:1-3 (NIV)

God not only allowed them to continue their foolishness but also caused them to be fooled by fallen angels who became demons parading as gods to the children of men.

The trend of demons claiming to be gods continued and became so bad that some religions' practices by some men identify with hundreds of gods. It is something close to the highest level of foolishness in man to imagine that it is acceptable for a man to simultaneously worship as many as two hundred gods.

The downward spiral of man continued until God deemed it time for the liberation of man. It was obvious that man could not help himself, hence the necessity of a superior being to rescue man.

Why couldn't any of the prophets be the sacrificial lamb? Among other reasons, just as an enslaved person cannot negotiate the liberty of another, so a condemned sinner cannot save another condemned sinner. Why not one of the mighty Angels? An angel cannot perfectly fit the role of living on earth and feeling pain like a man.

There was also the matter of what is now known as the event of the progeny of the sons of Anakim. The last time God permitted angels to relate closely with men, the result was the birth of abnormal hybrid beings contrary to the will of God. The giant beings were referred to as the sons of Anakim.

Who Was Anak in the Bible?

Anak, son of Arba, is the father of the Anakim race. Simple enough, what all do we know about him? Unfortunately, not very much. We only have references to his lineage:

In accordance with the Lord's command to him, Joshua gave to Caleb son of Jephunneh a portion in Judah—Kiriath Arba, that is, Hebron. (Arba was the forefather of Anak.)
Joshua 15:13 (NIV)

We know that Arba, Anak's father, led a city:

They gave them Kiriath Arba (that is, Hebron), with its surrounding pastureland, in the hill country of Judah. (Arba was the forefather of Anak.)
Joshua 21:11 (NIV)

Apart from that, we cannot dissect much about him from the biblical text.

Consequently, God himself was the only being who could slot perfectly into the role of saving man from his imminent destruction.

God had to come to the world in the form of a man to feel like a man, suffer as a man and die as a man. God eventually came as an extension of His self, whom we now identify as God the son.

The story of the salvation of mankind is a story of sacrifice, pain, and remarkable freedom. The world will never need such great freedom again as it was a once and forever event. Jesus Christ paid the final price for the salvation of mankind.

The next day John saw Jesus coming toward him and said, "Look, the Lamb of God, who takes away the sin of the world!
John 1:29 (NIV)

Fulfilling the Requirements for Salvation of Man.

15 For we do not have a high priest who is unable to empathize with our weaknesses, but we have one who has been tempted in every way, just as we are—yet he did not sin. 16 Let us then approach God's throne of grace with confidence, so that we may receive mercy and find grace to help us in our time of need.
Hebrews 4: 15-16 (NIV)

Man's salvation was achieved through the blood of our High Priest, who also doubled as the sacrificial lamb. He came as a man and fulfilled all the difficult requirements to perfection.

The first requirement was that the sacrificial being must be blameless from birth and be without sin. Jesus Christ fulfilled this by coming through the womb of a virgin. This means someone who had never experienced the corruption of intercourse with a man and standing as a symbol of spotless without blemish.

The breaking of the hymen of the Virgin Mary at the birth of Jesus Christ also signifies taintlessness. It is similar to the cutting of the ribbon at commissioning something new and hitherto unused.

Also, the submission of Jesus Christ to be sacrificed as a cover for the sin of man was a replica of an event in the Garden of Eden. After the fall of man, Adam and Eve tried helping themselves with their own wisdom. They got fig leaves to cover their shame. However, as a sign of God's eternal mercy and faithfulness, despite their sins, God still caused an innocent animal to die so the skin could be used to cover the nakedness of the two.

Also, to safeguard His blameless nature, Jesus Christ started His business from an early age. He declared His purpose early and stuck to it all His life. Another factor of note is His low-key lifestyle for the first thirty years of His life. He maintained a low-key life, hardly displaying His immense powers. At thirty, He was baptized and went straight to the wilderness to wait on God, the Father. After that, He selected His disciples, who were witnesses to His blameless life to this day.

The next great condition to be fulfilled by the sacrificial lamb who will take away the sins of the world was spreading the knowledge of the glory of God worldwide. You may wonder why this was necessary. The necessity will take us back to the period when the Israelites wandered in the wilderness after God delivered them from the Egyptians.

There was a need for the Israelites to know who God was and why He should be worshiped. When God revealed Himself to them, what they saw was His glory. That was what God made them see.

Nevertheless, as surely as I live and as surely as the glory of the Lord fills the whole earth,
Numbers 14:21 (NIV)

The result is that the Israelites only saw His glory. They had no knowledge or understanding of God, which resulted in many of them perishing.

My people are destroyed from lack of knowledge.
"Because you have rejected knowledge,
I also reject you as my priests;
because you have ignored the law of your God,
I also will ignore your children.
Hosea 4:6 (NIV)

The lack of knowledge of the God they were dealing with made them run afoul of His will, and many paid the ultimate price. There was then a necessity for man to see His glory and have a good knowledge of His glory. By the time of Isaiah, the prophet, God placed more emphasis on knowledge about Him. He sent the prophet Isaiah to say as much.

They will neither harm nor destroy
  on all my holy mountain,
for the earth will be filled with the knowledge of the Lord
  as the waters cover the sea.
Isaiah 11:9 (NIV)

As the knowledge of God grew, there was a need to streamline that knowledge back to the originally intended nature of God's relationship with man, which is for man to observe His glory and worship Him. This was made known in the days of prophet Habakkuk.

For the earth will be filled with the knowledge of the glory of the Lord as the waters cover the sea.
Habakkuk 2:14 (NIV)

Thus, the original plan of God was restored. However, there was still a need for the whole earth to taste this knowledge of God's awesomeness in glory. This then forms the second important requirement to be fulfilled by Jesus Christ.

For this to be fulfilled, Jesus Christ had to subject Himself to the required conditions for spiritual enablement. He fasted, prayed often, tarried in the presence of God the Father, and went out to propagate the gospel. He also consecrated Himself to keep His ministry from corruption.

Another unique thing about Jesus Christ that made Him stand perfect for the role of fulfilling the second requirement is His ability to shed a bit of Himself in the hearts of His disciples, thereby turning them into small Christs.

His disciples were able to go out after they had been endured with power from on high on Pentecost day. They were able to fulfill His mandate on them to go out and witness to all men, even to the uttermost parts of the world.

Therefore go and make disciples of all nations, baptizing them in the name of the Father and of the Son and of the Holy Spirit, 20 and teaching them to obey everything I have commanded you. And surely I am with you always, to the very end of the age."
Matthew 28:19-20 (NIV)

It must be noted that even at that, He had to hand over the continuous fulfillment of the requirement to the Holy Spirit. He left with a promise to send the Holy Spirit to continue the work of salvation among men.

One singular reason the Holy Spirit needed to come into the picture by empowering the disciple to witness and wrought miracles is that salvation is a continuous experience. That a man is saved does not mean that he is forever saved. Many were saved, but they later lost their salvation and slumped back to living the life of an unsaved man.

And I will ask the Father, and he will give you another advocate to help you and be with you forever—
John 14:16 (NIV)

But very truly, I tell you, it is for your good that I am going away. Unless I go away, the Advocate will not come to you; but if I go, I will send him to you.
John 16:7 (NIV)

But when he, the Spirit of truth, comes, he will guide you into all the truth. He will not speak on his own; he will speak only what he hears, and he will tell you what is yet to come.
John 16:13 (NIV)

The third requirement is that of a painful death. Another related condition is He must be paraded like a common thief and die like an accursed man. To fulfill this, He was wrongly accused, stripped naked, and beaten in public. Then he was paraded openly as he bore his cross to His place of crucifixion. He also died in a tree or crucifix, which is a curse. He became cursed to bear away the curse on Adam's helpless race. He endured pain to take away the pain of man. One irony about this part of the salvation story is that Jesus was beaten and made to suffer by the ones he came to save. The very ones He died for were the ones who killed Him. Jesus Christ died cursed and earned a place in hell rather than heaven when He died.

However, He wrestled His way back from hell by seizing the key of death from Satan. On the third day, He rose from the dead victorious, and many other souls rose with Him. The Psalmist testified of this long ago, how Jesus was able to win His return to life through the everlasting doors separating the living from the dead.

Lift up your heads, you gates;
  be lifted up, you ancient doors,
  that the King of glory may come in.

8 Who is this King of glory?
  The Lord strong and mighty,
  the Lord mighty in battle.

9 Lift up your heads, you gates;
  lift them up, you ancient doors,
  that the King of glory may come in.

10 Who is He, this King of glory?
  The Lord Almighty—
  He is the King of glory.

Psalms 24:7-10 (NIV)

Jesus Christ earned His right back to glory rather than curse by returning to life from the belly of hell. It was the ultimate sucker punch to the devil who thought he had the Prince of glory trapped in hell.

There were proofs that Jesus Christ rose again from the dead to perfect the process of man's salvation. There had been prophecies about the event which were documented. Also, when Jesus died, there was sudden darkness even though it was at three o clock in the afternoon.

The most significant proof, however, is the parting of the veil in the temple that separates the holy of holies or the innermost part from the rest of the temple. Not only did the veil tear in two, but it also tore from top to bottom, signifying three things.

The occurrence signifies acceptance of the sacrifice of Jesus Christ as the lamb who takes away the sins of the world.

The next day John saw Jesus coming toward him and said, "Look, the Lamb of God, who takes away the sin of the world!
John 1: 29 (NIV)

The veil tore to expose the temple's innermost part, signifying access to God without needing a mediator.

For the grace of God has appeared that offers salvation to all people.
Titus 2:11 (NIV)

That the veil tore from top to bottom tells of the grace for salvation coming down from heaven to earth.

And when Jesus had cried out again in a loud voice, he gave up his spirit.

51 At that moment the curtain of the temple was torn in two from top to bottom. The earth shook, the rocks split

52 and the tombs broke open. The bodies of many holy people who had died were raised to life.

53 They came out of the tombs after Jesus' resurrection and[a] went into the holy city and appeared to many people.

Matthew 27:50-53 (NIV)

Our God is a God of mercy. He is also a God of order; with Him, nothing just happens. In other words, there is always a reason and purpose for everything He permits. Glory be to Him in the highest, who has allowed salvation to come to us.

Chapter Eleven

After Salvation, What Next?

Therefore, I urge you, brothers, and sisters, in view of God's mercy, to offer your bodies as a living sacrifice, holy and pleasing to God—this is your true and proper worship. 2 Do not conform to the pattern of this world, but be transformed by the renewing of your mind. Then you will be able to test and approve what God's will is—his good, pleasing and perfect will.
Romans 12: 1-2 (NIV)

21 Do not be overcome by evil, but overcome evil with good.
Romans 12:21 (NIV)

The greatest mistake a new convert can make is to relax after the salvation experience.

Satan expects to see new converts rest on their oars after being saved and expect a joy ride to paradise. The Christian race is no child's play; the earlier a new convert is aware of this, the safer.

Salvation is important but what you do with your salvation is even more important. There are lots of instances of people who were saved from the darkness of godlessness but still manage to lose their salvation. Salvation can be lost.

My prayer for my Hindu family is that they experience true salvation and receive the grace to keep their salvation in Jesus' name. I pray a similar prayer for everyone reading this book that you will not lose your salvation in Jesus' mighty name.

After salvation, what is next? When a farmer plants a seed, his first expectation is for the seed to remain in the soil and not be picked by a bird or a rodent. Then he expects that seed to grow to become a whole plant. After which, he rightly expects the plant to bear fruits. God expectation concerning us is no different. He expects us to abide, grow, and bear good fruits.

ABIDE

Remain in me, as I also remain in you. No branch can bear fruit by itself; it must remain in the vine. Neither can you bear fruit unless you remain in me.

5 "I am the vine; you are the branches. If you remain in me and I in you, you will bear much fruit; apart from me you can do nothing.

6 If you do not remain in me, you are like a branch that is thrown away and withers; such branches are picked up, thrown into the fire and burned.

7 If you remain in me and my words remain in you, ask whatever you wish, and it will be done for you.
John 15:4-7 (NIV)

God wants you to abide in Christ. He does not expect you to try to grow in isolation but to grow in Christ. The period of abiding is the period of growing roots for a firm grip so that when storms of discouragement arise in the future, you might be able to withstand them all.

The Bible says:

For no one can lay any foundation other than the one already laid, which is Jesus Christ.
1 Corinthians 3:11 (NIV)

Your root as you abide must be intertwined in Christ Jesus for a solid foundation in Him. How do you grow roots in Christ Jesus? How do you abide in Him? There are several things to do to grow roots in Christ while we abide in Him. Some of them are listed below but not in any particular order as no two Christian races are ever the same. One way of growing in Christ is to learn more about Jesus Christ. Understand what He stands for and why! He came to die for your sin; that is when you can tell how you fit into His body.

Too many times, new converts come into Christ, still dragging their loads of worries from their past life. This can only slow down their growth or make them grow haphazardly. For instance, a convert who believes it is okay to participate in rituals in worship of other gods may grow and later teach future converts that such action is in order.

It is important to drop your burdens at the feet of Christ when you give your life to Jesus. You are expected to give both your life and your burdens to Him.

"Come to me, all you who are weary and burdened, and I will give you rest.

29 Take my yoke upon you and learn from me, for I am gentle and humble in heart, and you will find rest for your souls.
Matthew 11:28-29 (NIV)

According to the account above, Jesus Christ himself calls out to you to bring your burdens of worries, poverty, stagnation, and other earthly challenges to Him. He promises to give you rest from bearing these burdens. Then He asked that we take His yoke, which we shall look at later. His next instruction is to learn of Him. The period of abiding which follows salvation is the period of learning more about Jesus Christ.

Another expectation at this stage is to be baptized by water immersion than to wait on God for a baptism of the Holy Spirit. Baptism by immersion in a water body is a symbolic Christian ritual that signifies death to the world and coming to life on Jesus Christ. It should be done in the name of God the Father, God the Son, and God the Holy Ghost.

On the other hand, Holy Spirit baptism is not a human ritual but a divine encounter with the Holy Spirit. It is often followed by speaking in new tongues. Another sign of Holy Spirit baptism is an endowment with power from on high. Boldness also follows, among other gifts and virtues related to the Holy Spirit.

While abiding in Christ, you must earnestly ask for the baptism of the Holy Spirit, or else the devil may truncate your Christian journey. The Holy Spirit is the backbone of a Christian, without which our Christian experience is not complete.

After learning about Christ and receiving the Holy Spirit baptism, another critical thing to do is learn the Word of God. It is a time to study the Bible so as not to be swayed by every wind of doctrine.

Do your best to present yourself to God as one approved, a worker who does not need to be ashamed and who correctly handles the word of truth.
2 Timothy 2:15 (NIV)

When Christians maximize their abiding period, they grow well and know the truth. As a result, such Christians accurately divide the Word of Truth and cannot fall prey to Satan or any of his false prophets.

No wonder the psalmist refers to the Word of God as you

continue in your Christian journey.

Your word is a lamp for my feet,
  a light on my path.
Psalms 119:105 (NIV)

Another vital thing to note at this stage is the lure of your past life. Your past will come calling, temptation will arise, and Satan will try to pull you back into darkness.

It is a time to shun the world and its affairs and focus on God. The Christian race is a battleground and should not be taken for granted.

No one serving as a soldier gets entangled in civilian affairs but tries to please his commanding officer.
2 Timothy 2:4 (NIV)

Avoid godless chatter, because those who indulge in it will become more and more ungodly.
2 Timothy 2:16 (NIV)

Do not love the world or anything in the world. If anyone loves the world, love for the Father[a] is not in them.

16 For everything in the world—the lust of the flesh, the lust of the eyes, and the pride of life—comes not from the Father but from the world.

17 The world and its desires pass away, but whoever does the will of God

lives forever.
1 John 2:15-17 (NIV)

The period of abiding is the period to build your prayer life. There is no better person to tell you how to use an item than the manufacturer. There is, therefore, no better personality to teach you how to achieve the best with your life than the owner and maker of your life, God. The way to get this instruction from God, however, is through prayer. Hence prayer is essential in this period. Prayer at this period will also help you not to fall into the traps of temptation that the devil must set before you.

"Watch and pray so that you will not fall into temptation. The spirit is willing, but the flesh is weak."
Matthew 26:41 (NIV)

Paul in the Bible also admonishes that we always pray. Pray at every opportunity you have and over every situation, whether good or otherwise.

1 Pray without ceasing.
Thessalonians 5:17 (KJV)

Finally, one other important business to settle at this period of your Christian race is to know your calling in the body of Christ. There are different callings on the body of Christ, and you need to know yours to understand where you fit in.

You must understand the relationship between your gifts and

talents, your calling, and the ministry God has called you. The three are interrelated but different. One leads to the other, or rather, one is determined by the other, and a poor understanding of these three terms can make a Christian waste productive years in Christ chasing shadow.

Your gift or talent or what you know how to do points you to your calling or the assignment God has purposes for you. The office of carrying out that assignment is your ministry.

Many have failed to identify their gifts and end up missing their calling. Some have used the five senses, the need to be seen by the world, or the passion for wealth as a determinant of their choice of ministry. Such ministry cannot survive.

Now about the gifts of the Spirit, brothers, and sisters, I do not want you to be uninformed.
1 Corinthians 12:1 (NIV)

There are different kinds of gifts, but the same Spirit distributes them.

5 There are different kinds of service, but the same Lord.

6 There are different kinds of working, but in all of them and in everyone it is the same God at work.

7 Now to each one the manifestation of the Spirit is given for the common good.

8 To one there is given through the Spirit a message of wisdom, to another a message of knowledge by means of the same Spirit,

9 to another faith by the same Spirit, to another gifts of healing by that one Spirit,

10 to another miraculous powers, to another prophecy, to another distinguishing between spirits, to another speaking in different kinds of tongues, [a] and to still another the interpretation of tongues. [b]

11 All these are the work of one and the same Spirit, and he distributes them to each one, just as he determines.
Unity and Diversity in the Body

12 Just as a body, though one, has many parts, but all its many parts form one body, so it is with Christ.

1 Corinthians 12:4-12 (NIV)

Examples of those who had gifts that pointed them to their calling and their ministries abound in the Bible. David, for instance, acquired the gift of shepherding as a youth and the responsibilities of leadership as well. He grew up leading a gang of men, and his calling was to be a ruler. His ministry was his kingship role in Israel.

Samuel had the gift of hearing from God from his youth. His calling was to be a prophet and a priest over the people of Israel, and his ministry was that of prophecy.

Paul was passionate about persuading others and arguing

about whatever he believed; that was a gift. God called him to evangelize, and his ministry is evangelism.

You may have the gift of singing and song composition. Your calling may be singing, and your ministry will then be music evangelism.

You may have the gift of an orator with a passion for the word. Your calling may be preaching or teaching, and your ministry may be either preacher or teacher.

It is crucial you know on time where you belong in the body of Christ so you can focus on that and begin to grow accordingly.

How do you know where you belong in the body of Christ? It may be by revelation through the word of God, through vision, through natural interest, through what you know how to do, or through appointment.

Jesus knew His purpose early and got down to the business He was called to do early without wasting time. No wonder He is such a huge success.

When he was twelve years old, they went up to the festival, according to the custom.
Luke 2:42 (NIV)

When they did not find him, they went back to Jerusalem to look for him.

46 After three days they found him in the temple courts, sitting among the

teachers, listening to them and asking them questions.
Luke 2:45-46 (NIV)

The period of abiding is therefore critical and extremely sensitive in the Christian race. Many Christians who made a shipwreck of their faith missed it at this stage; the significance of this period cannot be overemphasized.

It is the foundation-building stage, determination of growth, the direction of growth, building a relationship with God, and knowing your role in the body of Christ.

GROW

until we all reach unity in the faith and in the knowledge of the Son of God and become mature, attaining to the whole measure of the fullness of Christ.

14 Then we will no longer be infants, tossed back and forth by the waves, and blown here and there by every wind of teaching and by the cunning and craftiness of people in their deceitful scheming.

15 Instead, speaking the truth in love, we will grow to become in every respect the mature body of him who is the head, that is, Christ.

16 From him the whole body, joined and held together by every supporting ligament, grows and builds itself up in love, as each part does its work.

Ephesians 4:13-16 (NIV)

THE NEXT STAGE AFTER ABIDING IS GROWING IN CHRIST

The next stage after abiding is the expected stage of growth. As a Christian, you owe God a responsibility to grow and to grow well.

Growth has to do with an increase, either in size or number. In this context, it is increasing in the measure of Christ. It is abounding in good standing before Christ.

Growth can be positive or negative. Positive growth is growth in line with the expectation of God on us. Any form of abounding or amassing that is not in line with the expectation of God on a Christian is negative growth.

Another interesting thing to note with growth is the importance of location. A good crop growing in the wrong field is a weed and will be uprooted. A stall of sugar cane growing on a maize farm is an aberration. In the same vein, developing a good gift in the wrong setting or a setting where it is not meant for is negative growth. Another form of negative growth is growth with a wrong motive. So, getting better at an activity in church does not automatically mean your growth is perfect or positive.

It is essential to say that the foundation of Christian growth is in tribulation and trials. Jesus Christ told His disciples to expect tribulations.

"I have told you these things, so that in me you may have peace. In this world you will have trouble. But take heart! I have overcome the world."
John 16:33 (NIV)

These afflictions we do not want to see or experience often usher us into our glory in Christ Jesus.

I consider that our present sufferings are not worth comparing with the glory that will be revealed in us.

19 For the creation waits in eager expectation for the children of God to be revealed.

Romans 8:18-19 (NIV)

For our light and momentary troubles are achieving for us an eternal glory that far outweighs them all.
2 Corinthians 4:17 (NIV)

An excellent example of someone who endured a cruel trial but came out abounding was Job. The Bible, however, recounts that his later end was better than his beginning.

After Job had prayed for his friends, the Lord restored his fortunes and gave him twice as much as he had before.
Job 42:10 (NIV)

The Lord blessed the latter part of Job's life more than the former part. He had fourteen thousand sheep, six thousand camels, a thousand yoke of oxen and a thousand donkeys.

Job 42:12 (NIV)

Activities that lead to growth in Christ include working for Him and prayerfully tarrying in His presence. As for many who sacrifice for Him, He lifts them up in every one of their endeavors.

All the heroes of faith listed in Hebrews 11:1-39 worked and were rewarded with diverse rewards.

Now faith is confidence in what we hope for and assurance about what we do not see.

2 This is what the ancients were commended for.

Hebrews 11:1-2 (NIV)

Meditating on the word of God is another certain avenue to growth in Christ. Apostle Peter compares our expected desire for the word of God to the desire of a baby for milk. Then he clearly states that the word may aid our growth.

Therefore, rid yourselves of all malice and all deceit, hypocrisy, envy, and slander of every kind.

2 Like newborn babies, crave pure spiritual milk, so that by it you may grow up in your salvation,

1 Peter 2:1-2 (NIV)

The most significant hurdle to scale to attain growth is

withstanding trials, and if God is silent in your days of trial, it is because the teacher is always silent during a test.

Jesus made it clear that Christians shall face trials and tribulations in the world.

"I have told you these things, so that in me you may have peace. In this world you will have trouble. But take heart! I have overcome the world."
John 16:33 (NIV)

Trials and tribulation, therefore, are normal features of the Christian race.

When trials come your way, it is a sign that God reckons with you. It also signifies that the devil and his cohorts have marked you as a threat. But the Bible admonishes that you be of good cheer, for Jesus has overcome the world on your behalf.

In fact, everyone who wants to live a godly life in Christ Jesus will be persecuted,
2 Timothy 3:12 (NIV)

if we endure,
  we will also reign with him.

If we disown him,
  he will also disown us;

2 Timothy 2:12 (NIV)

Heaven established that trials must come; what do you do when trials come? You must learn to be like an eagle who rejoices in the face of storms.

Be joyful in hope, patient in affliction, faithful in prayer.
Romans 12:12 (NIV)

When trials come, you must remember they cannot last forever. Rejoice in the hope of a victorious tomorrow, be patient through the period of tribulation and be fervently in prayer for God to see you through. Our God is not an author of confusion.

As a soldier for Christ, you must be firm in the face of trials. Job, at the height of his trial, declared:

I know that my redeemer[a] lives,
　　and that in the end he will stand on the earth. [b]
Job 19:25 (NIV)

Earlier, Job declares:

Though he slay me, yet will I hope in him;
　　I will surely[a] defend my ways to his face.
Job 13:15 (NIV)

This is the stand of a true child of God. No matter how bad the situation, stay firm in the Lord and earn your place as a hero of faith.

When trials come, you must learn to trust God. Put your trust in Him, and your trial will lose its potency. The arm of flesh will fail you; your knowledge will fail you, and your understanding will not suffice. All you must do is trust God with your all.

Trust in the Lord with all your heart
*   and lean not on your own understanding;*

6 in all your ways submit to him,
*   and he will make your paths straight. [a]*

7 Do not be wise in your own eyes;
*   fear the Lord and shun evil.*

Proverbs 3:5-7 (NIV)

The best place to be in times of difficulty is with God.

Whoever dwells in the shelter of the Most High
*   will rest in the shadow of the Almighty. [a]*

2 I will say of the Lord, "He is my refuge and my fortress,
*   my God, in whom I trust."*

3 Surely he will save you
*   from the fowler's snare*
*   and from the deadly pestilence.*

Psalms 91:1-3 (NIV)

Finally, after the period of abiding and growing, there is one more stage for a child of God to pass through. It is the stage of fruit-bearing.

BEAR FRUIT

Just as a well-developed crop is useless without bearing fruit, a Christian is ineffective without bearing fruits.

He cuts off every branch in me that bears no fruit, while every branch that does bear fruit he prunes[a] so that it will be even more fruitful.
John 15:2 (NIV)

"I am the vine; you are the branches. If you remain in me and I in you, you will bear much fruit; apart from me you can do nothing.
John 15:5 (NIV)

This is to my Father's glory, that you bear much fruit, showing yourselves to be my disciples.
John 15:8 (NIV)

Fruit-bearing is necessary for a child of God. What type of fruits does God expect from you? He expects fruits that lead to abundant life in the nearer as well as the souls he wins into the body of Christ.

The fruit of the righteous is a tree of life,
   and the one who is wise saves lives.
Proverbs 11:30 (NIV)

As the Bible portion above noted, winning souls is wise, and it is one of the ways we bear fruit in Christ.

Those who are wise[a] will shine like the brightness of the heavens, and those who lead many to righteousness, like the stars for ever and ever.
Daniel 12:3 (NIV)

Those who convert others from their wrong ways are wise and shall shine in glory.

Another way of bearing fruit is by living a life of example. Let others see Jesus in you. Let your conduct bring men to God. Let your presence be a blessing to people around you.

The Apostle Paul preaches:

Therefore I urge you to imitate me.
1 Corinthians 4:16 (NIV)

Follow my example, as I follow the example of Christ.
1 Corinthians 11:1 (NIV)

Like Apostle Paul, we should imitate Christ as He imitated His Father. Like Apostle Paul's, your life should be a worthy example to people around you. Finally, you should abound in good works. In this way, you will fulfill the will of God for your life.

This is my wish for my family: that they know the only true God and accept Christ. Also, I wish they will abide, grow, and bear good fruits in Christ. I pray for everyone reading this book that you will experience God anew in Jesus' name. You will abide in Him, grow, and bear wonderful fruits in the awesome name of Jesus. Amen!

10 POWERFUL PRAYERS FOR DELIVERANCE

Psalms 32:7 (NIV)
You are my hiding place;
*   you will protect me from trouble*
*   and surround me with songs of deliverance.*

Prayer: Father, disperse every trouble surrounding me today and fill my tongue with songs of deliverance. Amen

Psalms 34:4 (NIV)
I sought the Lord, and he answered me;
*   he delivered me from all my fears.*

Prayer: As I pray to you today, answer and deliver me from all my fears and worries. Amen

Psalms 40:13 (NIV)
Be pleased to save me, Lord;
*   come quickly, Lord, to help me.*

Prayer: O Lord, let it please you to deliver me from every demonic attack and influence of false religions over my life. Amen

Psalm 50:15 (NIV)
and call on me in the day of trouble;
*   I will deliver you, and you will honor me."*

Prayer: Deliver me from the powers of darkness; let them not have dominion over me, and I will glorify you. Amen

Psalms 107:6 (NIV)
Then they cried out to the Lord in their trouble,
  and he delivered them from their distress.

Prayer: Every arrow of distress aimed against my soul; I decree that they go back to their senders. Amen

James 4:7 (NIV)
Submit yourselves, then, to God. Resist the devil, and he will flee from you.

Prayer: Every satanic agent hovering around my children be bounded forever. Amen

James 5:16 (NIV)
Therefore confess your sins to each other and pray for each other so that you may be healed. The prayer of a righteous person is powerful and effective.

Prayer: Every area of my life that needs your healing, be it my health, finance, relationship, etc., let your healing Hand rest upon them. Amen

John 15:7 (NIV)
If you remain in me and my words remain in you, ask whatever you wish, and it will be done for you.

Prayer: Father, I decree that my next level has arrived in Jesus'

name. Every spirit of stagnation and refrigeration around my life is forever banished in Jesus' name. Amen

Psalms 34:19-20 (NIV)

The righteous person may have many troubles,
   but the Lord delivers him from them all;

20 he protects all his bones,
   not one of them will be broken.

Prayer: Deliver me, Father, from every affliction warring against my life. Keep all my sources of support safe. Amen

John 8:32 (NIV)

Then you will know the truth, and the truth will set you free."

Prayer: Father, every truth needed for my liberation from darkness, send them to me today. Amen

ABOUT THE AUTHOR

Barbara Buononato was born in Guyana, SA, and was raised outside the city of New York, in the beautiful Hudson Valley, State of New Paltz. Barbara considers her faith and family to be most important to her. If she isn't spending time with her husband and family, you can always find her around her garden.

This is a must-read for every believer, those seeking a deeper relationship with God, and is a blessing to the body of Christ.

A NOTE FROM THE AUTHOR:

I am a very personalized first-time writer that's led by The Holy Spirit. I like being able to make my writing something other people can connect to collect.

I have a strong relationship with the WRITTEN WORD that I enjoy elaborating on minor details with a plethora of information.

This book is my first written work and I hope it blesses you as much as it has ministered to me.

In His Presence,

Barbara Buononato